THE GARDEN OF
THE PROPHET

"His power came from some great reservoir of spiritual life else it could not have been so universal and so potent, but the majesty and beauty of the language with which he clothed it were all his own."   —CLAUDE BRAGDON

THE BOOKS OF
KAHLIL GIBRAN

The Madman 1918

The Forerunner 1920

The Prophet 1923

Sand and Foam 1927

Jesus, the Son of Man 1928

The Earth Gods 1931

The Wanderer 1932

The Garden of the Prophet 1933

Prose Poems 1934

Nymphs of the Valley 1948

Spirits Rebellious 1949

A Tear and a Smile 1950

The Broken Wings 1959

The Voice of the Master 1960

A Self-Portrait 1960

Thoughts and Meditations 1961

Spiritual Sayings 1963

THE GARDEN OF
THE PROPHET

BY
KAHLIL GIBRAN

HEINEMANN : LONDON

William Heinemann Ltd
15 Queen Street, Mayfair, London W1X 8BE

LONDON   MELBOURNE   TORONTO
JOHANNESBURG   AUCKLAND

First published 1934
This edition 1954
Reprinted 1957, 1961, 1964, 1968, 1970, 1972
Reset 1974

434 29063 7

Printed by:
Kustannusosakeyhtiö Otava Keuruu Finland
1974
Member of Finnprint

THE FIVE ILLUSTRATIONS
IN THIS VOLUME
ARE REPRODUCED FROM
ORIGINAL DRAWINGS
BY THE AUTHOR.
THE TWO PAGES OF FACSIMILE
ON PAGES 20 AND 21
ARE REPRODUCED FROM
THE ORIGINAL MANUSCRIPT

ALMUSTAFA, the chosen and the beloved, who was a noon unto his own day, returned to the isle of his birth in the month of Tichreen, which is the month of remembrance.

And as his ship approached the harbour, he stood upon its prow, and his mariners were about him. And there was a homecoming in his heart.

And he spoke, and the sea was in his voice, and he said: "Behold, the isle of our birth. Even here the earth heaved us, a song and a riddle; a song unto the sky, a riddle unto the earth; and what is there between earth and sky that shall carry the song and solve the riddle save our own passion?

"The sea yields us once more to these shores. We are but another wave of her waves. She sends us forth to sound her speech, but how shall we do so unless we break the symmetry of our heart on rock and sand?

"For this is the law of mariners and the sea: If you would freedom, you must needs turn to mist. The formless is for ever seeking form, even as the countless nebulæ would become suns and moons; and we who have sought much and return now to the isle, rigid moulds, we must become mist once more and learn of the beginning. And what is there that shall

I

live and rise unto the heights except it be broken unto passion and freedom?

"For ever shall we be in quest of the shores, that we may sing and be heard. But what of the wave that breaks where no ear shall hear? It is the unheard in us that nurses our deeper sorrow. Yet it is also the unheard which carves our soul to form and fashions our destiny."

Then one of his mariners came forth and said: "Master, you have captained our longing for this harbour, and behold, we have come. Yet you speak of sorrow, and of hearts that shall be broken."

And he answered him and said: "Did I not speak of freedom, and of the mist which is our greater freedom? Yet it is in pain I make pilgrimage to the isle where I was born, even like unto a ghost of one slain come to kneel before those who have slain him."

And another mariner spoke and said: "Behold, the multitudes on the sea-wall. In their silence they have foretold even the day and the hour of your coming, and they have gathered from their fields and vineyards in their loving need, to await you."

And Almustafa looked afar upon the multitudes, and his heart was mindful of their yearning, and he was silent.

Then a cry came from the people, and it was a cry of remembrance and of entreaty.

And he looked upon his mariners and said: "And what have I brought them? A hunter was I, in a distant land. With aim and might I have spent the golden arrows they gave me, but I have brought down no game. I followed not the arrows. Mayhap they are spreading now in the sun with the pinions of wounded eagles that would not fall to earth. And mayhap the arrowheads have fallen into the hands of those who had need of them for bread and wine.

"I know not where they have spent their flight, but this I know: they have made their curve in the sky.

"Even so, love's hand is still upon me, and you, my mariners, still sail my vision, and I shall not be dumb. I shall cry out when the hand of the seasons is upon my throat, and I shall sing my words when my lips are burned with flames."

And they were troubled in their hearts because he spoke these things. And one said: "Master, teach us all, and mayhap because your blood flows in our veins, and our breath is of your fragrance, we shall understand."

Then he answered them, and the wind was in his voice, and he said: "Brought you me to the isle of my birth to be a teacher? Not yet have I been caged by wisdom. Too young am I and too verdant to speak of aught but self, which is for ever the deep calling upon the deep.

"Let him who would have wisdom seek it in the buttercup or in a pinch of red clay. I am still the singer. Still I shall sing the earth, and I shall sing your lost dreaming that walks the day between sleep and sleep. But I shall gaze upon the sea."

. . . . .

And now the ship entered the harbour and reached the sea-wall, and he came thus to the isle of his birth and stood once more amongst his own people. And a great cry arose from their hearts so that the loneliness of his home-coming was shaken within him.

And they were silent awaiting his word, but he answered them not, for the sadness of memory was upon him, and he said in his heart: "Have I said that I shall sing? Nay, I can but open my lips that the voice of life may come forth and go out to the wind for joy and support."

Then Karima, she who had played with him, a child, in the Garden of his mother, spoke and said: "Twelve years have you hidden your face from us, and for twelve years have we hungered and thirsted for your voice."

And he looked upon her with exceeding tenderness, for it was she who had closed the eyes of his mother when the white wings of death had gathered her.

And he answered and said: "Twelve years? Said you twelve years, Karima? I measured not my longing with the starry rod, nor did I sound the depth thereof. For love when love is homesick exhausts time's measurements and time's soundings.

"There are moments that hold æons of separation. Yet parting is naught but an exhaustion of the mind. Perhaps we have not parted."

And Almustafa looked upon the people, and he saw them all, the youth and the aged, the stalwart and the puny, those who were ruddy with the touch of wind and sun, and those also who were of pallid countenance; and upon their face a light of longing and of questioning.

And one spoke and said: "Master, life has dealt bitterly with our hopes and our desires. Our hearts are troubled, and we do not understand. I pray you, comfort us, and open to us the meanings of our sorrows."

And his heart was moved with compassion, and he said: "Life is older than all things living; even as beauty was wingèd ere the beautiful was born on earth, and even as truth was truth ere it was uttered.

"Life sings in our silences, and dreams in our slumber. Even when we are beaten and low, Life is enthroned and high. And when we weep, Life smiles upon the day, and is free even when we drag our chains.

"Oftentimes we call Life bitter names, but only when we ourselves are bitter and dark. And we deem her empty and unprofitable, but only when the soul goes wandering in desolate places, and the heart is drunken with overmindfulness of self.

"Life is deep and high and distant; and though only your vast vision can reach even her feet, yet she is near; and though only the breath of your breath reaches her heart, the shadow of your shadow crosses her face, and the echo of your faintest cry becomes a spring and an autumn in her breast.

"And Life is veiled and hidden, even as your greater self is hidden and veiled. Yet when Life speaks, all the winds become words; and when she

5

speaks again, the smiles upon your lips and the tears in your eyes turn also into words. When she sings, the deaf hear and are held; and when she comes walking, the sightless behold her and are amazed and follow her in wonder and astonishment."

And he ceased from speaking, and a vast silence enfolded the people, and in the silence there was an unheard song, and they were comforted of their loneliness and their aching.

AND he left them straightway and followed the path which led to his Garden, which was the Garden of his mother and his father, wherein they lay asleep, they and their forefathers.

And there were those who would have followed after him, seeing that it was a homecoming, and he was alone, for there was not one left of all his kin to spread the feast of welcome, after the manner of his people.

But the captain of his ship counselled them saying: "Suffer him to go upon his way. For his bread is the bread of aloneness, and in his cup is the wine of remembrance, which he would drink alone."

And his mariners held their steps, for they knew it was even as the captain of the ship had told them. And all those who gathered upon the sea-wall restrained the feet of their desire.

Only Karima went after him, a little way, yearning over his aloneness and his memories. And she spoke not, but turned and went unto her own house, and in the garden under the almond tree she wept, yet knew not wherefore.

AND Almustafa came and found the Garden of his mother and his father, and he entered in, and closed the gate that no man might come after him.

And for forty days and forty nights he dwelt alone in that house and that Garden, and none came, not even unto the gate, for it was closed, and all the people knew that he would be alone.

And when the forty days and nights were ended, Almustafa opened the gate that they might come in.

And there came nine men to be with him in the Garden; three mariners from his own ship; three who had served in the Temple; and three who had been his comrades in play when they were but children together. And these were his disciples.

And on a morning his disciples sat around him, and there were distances and remembrances in his eyes. And that disciple who was called Hafiz said unto him: "Master, tell us of the city of Orphalese, and of that land wherein you tarried those twelve years."

And Almustafa was silent, and he looked away toward the hills and toward the vast ether, and there was a battle in his silence.

Then he said: "My friends and my road-fellows,

pity the nation that is full of beliefs and empty of religion.

"Pity the nation that wears a cloth it does not weave, eats a bread it does not harvest, and drinks a wine that flows not from its own wine-press.

"Pity the nation that acclaims the bully as hero, and that deems the glittering conqueror bountiful.

"Pity a nation that despises a passion in its dream, yet submits in its awakening.

"Pity the nation that raises not its voice save when it walks in a funeral, boasts not except among its ruins, and will rebel not save when its neck is laid between the sword and the block.

"Pity the nation whose statesman is a fox, whose philosopher is a juggler, and whose art is the art of patching and mimicking.

"Pity the nation that welcomes its new ruler with trumpetings, and farewells him with hootings, only to welcome another with trumpetings again.

"Pity the nation whose sages are dumb with years and whose strong men are yet in the cradle.

"Pity the nation divided into fragments, each fragment deeming itself a nation."

AND one said: "Speak to us of that which is moving in your own heart even now."

And he looked upon that one, and there was in his voice a sound like a star singing, and he said: "In your waking dream, when you are hushed and listening to your deeper self, your thoughts, like snowflakes, fall and flutter and garment all the sounds of your spaces with white silence.

"And what are waking dreams but clouds that bud and blossom on the sky-tree of your heart? And what are your thoughts but the petals which the winds of your heart scatter upon the hills and its fields?

"And even as you wait for peace until the formless within you takes form, so shall the cloud gather and drift until the Blessed Fingers shape its grey desire to little crystal suns and moon and stars."

Then Sarkis, he who was the half-doubter, spoke and said: "But spring shall come, and all the snows of our dreams and our thoughts shall melt and be no more."

And he answered, saying: "When Spring comes to seek His beloved among the slumbering groves and vineyards, the snows shall indeed melt and shall run in streams to seek the river in the valley, to be the cup-bearer to the myrtle-trees and laurel.

"So shall the snow of your heart melt when your Spring is come, and thus shall your secret run in streams to seek the river of life in the valley. And the river shall enfold your secret and carry it to the great sea.

"All things shall melt and turn into songs when Spring comes. Even the stars, the vast snow-flakes that fall slowly upon the larger fields, shall melt into singing streams. When the sun of His face shall arise above the wider horizon, then what frozen symmetry would not turn into liquid melody? And who among you would not be cup-bearer to the myrtle and the laurel?

"It was but yesterday that you were moving with the moving sea, and you were shoreless and without a self. Then the wind, the breath of Life, wove you, a veil of light on her face; then her hand gathered you and gave you form, and with a head held high you sought the heights. But the sea followed after you, and her song is still with you. And though you have forgotten your parentage, she will for ever assert her motherhood, and for ever will she call you unto her.

"In your wanderings among the mountains and the desert you will always remember the depth of her cool heart. And though oftentimes you will not know for what you long, it is indeed for her vast and rhythmic peace.

"And how else can it be? In grove and in bower when the rain dances in leaves upon the hill, when snow falls, a blessing and a covenant; in the valley when you lead your flocks to the river; in your fields where brooks, like silver streams, join together the green garment; in your gardens when the early dews mirror the heavens; in your meadows when the mist of evening half veils your way; in all these the sea is with you, a witness to your heritage, and a claim upon your love.

"It is the snow-flake in you running down to the sea."

AND on a morning as they walked in the Garden, there appeared before the gate a woman, and it was Karima, she whom Almustafa had loved even as a sister in his boyhood. And she stood without, asking nothing, nor knocking with her hand upon the gate, but only gazing with longing and sadness into the Garden.

And Almustafa saw the desire upon her eyelids, and with swift steps he came to the wall and the gate and opened unto her, and she came in and was made welcome.

And she spoke and said: "Wherefore have you withdrawn yourself from us altogether, that we may not live in the light of your countenance? For behold, these many years have we loved you and waited with longing for your safe return. And now the people cry for you and would have speech with you; and I am their messenger come to beseech you that you will show yourself to the people, and speak to them out of your wisdom, and comfort the broken of heart and instruct our foolishness."

And looking upon her, he said: "Call me not wise unless you call all men wise. A young fruit am I, still clinging to the branch, and it was only yesterday that I was but a blossom.

"And call none among you foolish, for in truth we are neither wise nor foolish. We are green leaves upon the tree of life, and life itself is beyond wisdom, and surely beyond foolishness.

"And have I indeed withdrawn myself from you? Know you not that there is no distance save that which the soul does not span in fancy? And when the soul shall span that distance, it becomes a rhythm in the soul.

"The space that lies between you and your near neighbour unbefriended is indeed greater than that which lies between you and your beloved who dwells beyond seven lands and seven seas.

"For in remembrance there are no distances; and only in oblivion is there a gulf that neither your voice nor your eye can abridge.

"Between the shores of the oceans and the summit of the highest mountain there is a secret road which you must needs travel ere you become one with the sons of the earth.

"And between your knowledge and your under-standing there is a secret path which you must needs discover ere you become one with man, and there-fore one with yourself.

"Between your right hand that gives and your left hand that receives there is a great space. Only by deeming them both giving and receiving can you bring them into spacelessness, for it is only in knowing that you have naught to give and naught to receive that you can overcome space.

"Verily the vastest distance is that which lies

between your sleep-vision and your wakefulness; and between that which is but a deed and that which is a desire.

"And there is still another road which you must needs travel ere you become one with Life. But of that road I shall not speak now, seeing that you are weary already of travelling."

THEN he went forth with the woman, he and the nine, even unto the market-place, and he spoke to the people, his friends and his neighbours, and there was joy in their hearts and upon their eyelids.

And he said: "You grow in sleep, and live your fuller life in your dreaming. For all your days are spent in thanksgiving for that which you have received in the stillness of the night.

"Oftentimes you think and speak of night as the season of rest, yet in truth night is the season of seeking and finding.

"The day gives unto you the power of knowledge and teaches your fingers to become versed in the art of receiving; but it is night that leads you to the treasure-house of Life.

"The sun teaches to all things that grow their longing for the light. But it is night that raises them to the stars.

"It is indeed the stillness of the night that weaves a wedding-veil over the trees in the forest, and the flowers in the garden, and then spreads the lavish feast and makes ready the nuptial chamber; and in that holy silence tomorrow is conceived in the womb of Time.

"Thus it is with you, and thus, in seeking, you find meat and fulfilment. And though at dawn your awakening erases the memory, the board of dreams is for ever spread, and the nuptial chamber waiting."

And he was silent for a space, and they also, awaiting his word. Then he spoke again, saying: "You are spirits though you move in bodies; and, like oil that burns in the dark, you are flames though held in lamps.

"If you were naught save bodies, then my standing before you and speaking unto you would be but emptiness, even as the dead calling unto the dead. But this is not so. All that is deathless in you is free unto the day and the night and cannot be housed nor fettered, for this is the will of the Most High. You are His breath even as the wind that shall be neither caught nor caged. And I also am the breath of His breath."

And he went from their midst walking swiftly and entered again into the Garden.

And Sarkis, he who was the half-doubter, spoke and said: "And what of ugliness, Master? You speak never of ugliness."

And Almustafa answered him, and there was a whip in his words, and he said: "My friend, what man shall call you inhospitable if he shall pass by your house, yet would not knock at your door?

"And who shall deem you deaf and unmindful if

ان الشمس في قطرة الندى لا تقل عن الشمس — قطرات الندى

Dew-drops

The image of the morning sun in
a dew drop is not less than the
sun

The reflection of life in your
soul is not less than life.

A dew drop mirrors the
light because it is one with
light,

And you reflect life because
you and life are one.

When darkness is upon
you say " This darkness is
dawn not yet born

" And though night's
child bearing is upon me and
night's child birth shall be
upon me,

" Yet shall dawn be born

unto me,

Even as unto the hills and the valleys."

A dew drop rounding its sphere in the dusk of the lily is not unlike yourself gathering your soul in the heart of God.

Shall a dew drop say:

"But once in a thousand years am even a dew drop?"

And knows not that all light (of all the years) is shining in its circle.

— o —

he shall speak to you in a strange tongue of which you understand nothing?

"Is it not that which you have never striven to reach, into whose heart you have never desired to enter, that you deem ugliness?

"If ugliness is aught, indeed, it is but the scales upon our eyes, and the wax filling our ears.

"Call nothing ugly, my friend, save the fear of a soul in the presence of its own memories."

AND upon a day as they sat in the long shadows of the white poplars, one spoke, saying: "Master, I am afraid of time. It passes over us and robs us of our youth, and what does it give in return?"

And he answered and said: "Take up now a handful of good earth. Do you find in it a seed, and perhaps a worm? If your hand were spacious and enduring enough, the seed might become a forest, and the worm a flock of angels. And forget not that the years which turn seeds to forests, and worms to angels, belong to this *Now*, all of the years, this very *Now*.

"And what are the seasons of the years save your own thoughts changing? Spring is an awakening in your breast, and summer but a recognition of your own fruitfulness. Is not autumn the ancient in you singing a lullaby to that which is still a child in your being? And what, I ask you, is winter save sleep big with the dreams of all the other seasons."

And then Mannus, the inquisitive disciple, looked about him and he saw plants in flower cleaving unto the sycamore-tree. And he said: "Behold the parasites, Master. What say you of them? They are thieves with weary eyelids who steal the light from the steadfast children of the sun, and make fair of the sap that runneth into their branches and their leaves."

And he answered him saying: "My friend, we are all parasites. We who labour to turn the sod into pulsing life are not above those who receive life directly from the sod without knowing the sod.

"Shall a mother say to her child: 'I give you back to the forest, which is your greater mother, for you weary me, heart and hand'?

"Or shall the singer rebuke his own song, saying: 'Return now to the cave of echoes from whence you came, for your voice consumes my breath'?

"And shall the shepherd say to his yearling: 'I have no pasture whereunto I may lead you; therefore be cut off and become a sacrifice for this cause'?

"Nay, my friend, all these things are answered even before they are asked, and, like your dreams, are fulfilled ere you sleep.

"We live upon one another according to the law, ancient and timeless. Let us live thus in loving-kindness. We seek one another in our aloneness, and we walk the road when we have no hearth to sit beside.

"My friends and my brothers, the wider road is your fellow-man.

"These plants that live upon the tree draw the milk of the earth in the sweet stillness of night, and the earth in her tranquil dreaming sucks at the breast of the sun.

"And the sun, even as you and I and all there is, sits in equal honour at the banquet of the Prince whose door is always open and whose board is always spread.

"Mannus, my friend, all there is lives always upon all there is; and all there is lives in the faith, shoreless, upon the bounty of the Most High."

AND on a morning when the sky was yet pale with dawn, they walked all together in the Garden and looked unto the East and were silent in the presence of the rising sun.

And after a while Almustafa pointed with his hand, and he said: "The image of the morning sun in a dewdrop is not less than the sun. The reflection of life in your soul is not less than life.

"The dewdrop mirrors the light because it is one with light, and you reflect life because you and life are one.

"When darkness is upon you, say: 'This darkness is dawn not yet born; and though night's travail be full upon me, yet shall dawn be born unto me even as unto the hills.'

"The dewdrop rounding its sphere in the dusk of the lily is not unlike yourself gathering your soul in the heart of God.

"Shall a dewdrop say: 'But once in a thousand years am I even a dewdrop,' speak you and answer it, saying: 'Know you not that the light of all the years is shining in your circle?'"

AND on an evening a great storm visited the place, and Almustafa and his disciples, the nine, went within and sat about the fire and were still and silent.

Then one of the disciples said: "I am alone, Master, and the hoofs of the hours beat heavily upon my breast."

And Almustafa rose up and stood in their midst, and he said in a voice like unto the sound of a great wind: "Alone! And what of it? You came alone, and alone shall you pass into the mist.

"Therefore drink your cup alone and in silence. The autumn days have given other lips other cups and filled them with wine bitter and sweet, even as they have filled your cup.

"Drink your cup alone though it taste of your own blood and tears, and praise life for the gift of thirst. For without thirst your heart is but the shore of a barren sea, songless and without a tide.

"Drink your cup alone, and drink it with cheers.

"Raise it high above your head and drink deep to those who drink alone.

"Once I sought the company of men and sat with them at their banquet-tables and drank deep with them; but their wine did not rise to my head, nor did it flow into my bosom. It only descended to my feet.

27

My wisdom was left dry and my heart was locked and sealed. Only my feet were with them in their fog.

"And I sought the company of men no more, nor drank wine with them at their board.

"Therefore I say unto you, though the hoofs of the hours beat heavily upon your bosom, what of it? It is well for you to drink your cup of sorrow alone, and your cup of joy shall you drink alone also."

AND on a day, as Phardrous, the Greek, walked in the Garden, he struck his foot upon a stone and he was angered. And he turned and picked up the stone, saying in a low voice: "Oh dead thing in my path!" and he flung away the stone.

And Almustafa, the chosen and the beloved, said: "Why say you: 'O dead thing'? Have you been thus long in this Garden and know not that there is nothing dead here? All things live and glow in the knowledge of the day and the majesty of the night. You and the stone are one. There is a difference only in heart-beats. Your heart beats a little faster, does it, my friend? Ay, but it is not so tranquil.

"Its rhythm may be another rhythm, but I say unto you that if you sound the depths of your soul and scale the heights of space, you shall hear but one melody, and in that melody the stone and the star sing, the one with the other, in perfect unison.

"If my words reach not your understanding, then let be until another dawn. If you have cursed this stone because in your blindness you have stumbled upon it, then would you curse a star if so be your head should encounter it in the sky. But the day will come when you will gather stones and stars as a child plucks the valley-lilies, and then shall you know that all these things are living and fragrant."

AND on the first day of the week when the sounds of the temple bells sought their ears, one spoke and said: "Master, we hear much talk of God hereabout. What say you of God, and who is He in very truth?"

And he stood before them like a young tree, fearless of wind or tempest, and he answered saying: "Think now, my comrades and beloved, of a heart that contains all your hearts, a love that encompasses all your loves, a spirit that envelops all your spirits, a voice enfolding all your voices, and a silence deeper than all your silences, and timeless.

"Seek now to perceive in your self-fullness a beauty more enchanting than all things beautiful, a song more vast than the songs of the sea and the forest, a majesty seated upon a throne for which Orion is but a footstool, holding a sceptre in which the Pleiades are naught save the glimmer of dewdrops.

"You have sought always only food and shelter, a garment and a staff; seek now One who is neither an aim for your arrows nor a stony cave to shield you from the elements.

"And if my words are a rock and a riddle, then seek, none the less, that your hearts may be broken, and that your questionings may bring you unto the love and the wisdom of the Most High, whom men call God."

And they were silent, every one, and they were perplexed in their heart; and Almustafa was moved with compassion for them, and he gazed with tenderness upon them and said: "Let us speak no more now of God the Father. Let us speak rather of the gods, your neighbours, and of your brothers, the elements that move about your houses and your fields.

"You would rise in fancy unto the cloud, and you deem it height; and you would pass over the vast sea and claim it to be distance. But I say unto you that when you sow a seed in the earth, you reach a greater height; and when you hail the beauty of the morning to your neighbour, you cross a greater sea.

"Too often do you sing God, the Infinite, and yet in truth you hear not the song. Would that you might listen to the song-birds, and to the leaves that forsake the branch when the wind passes by, and forget not, my friends, that these sing only when they are separated from the branch!

"Again I bid you to speak not so freely of God, who is your All, but speak rather and understand one another, neighbour unto neighbour, a god unto a god.

"For what shall feed the fledgling in the nest if the mother bird flies skyward? And what anemone in the field shall be fulfilled unless it be husbanded by a bee from another anemone?

33

"It is only when you are lost in your smaller selves that you seek the sky which you call God. Would that you might find paths into your vast selves; would that you might be less idle and pave the roads!

"My mariners and my friends, it were wiser to speak less of God, whom we cannot understand, and more of each other, whom we may understand. Yet I would have you know that we are the breath and the fragrance of God. We are God, in leaf, in flower, and oftentimes in fruit."

AND on a morning when the sun was high, one of the disciples, one of those three who had played with him in childhood, approached him saying: "Master, my garment is worn, and I have no other. Give me leave to go unto the market-place and bargain, that perchance I may procure me new raiment."

And Almustafa looked upon the young man, and he said: "Give me your garment." And he did so and stood naked in the noonday.

And Almustafa said in a voice that was like a young steed running upon a road: "Only the naked live in the sun. Only the artless ride the wind. And he alone who loses his way a thousand times shall have a home-coming.

"The angels are tired of the clever. And it was but yesterday that an angel said to me: 'We created hell for those who glitter. What else but fire can erase a shining surface and melt a thing to its core?'

"And I said: 'But in creating hell you created devils to govern hell.' But the angel answered: 'Nay, hell is governed by those who do not yield to fire.'

"Wise angel! He knows the ways of men and the ways of half-men. He is one of the seraphim who come to minister unto the prophets when they are

35

tempted by the clever. And no doubt he smiles when the prophets smile, and weeps also when they weep.

"My friends and my mariners, only the naked live in the sun. Only the rudderless can sail the greater sea. Only he who is dark with the night shall wake with the dawn, and only he who sleeps with the roots under the snow shall reach the spring.

"For you are even like roots, and like roots are you simple, yet you have wisdom from the earth. And you are silent, yet you have within your unborn branches the choir of the four winds.

"You are frail and you are formless, yet you are the beginning of giant oaks, and of the half-pencilled pattern of the willows against the sky.

"Once more I say, you are but roots betwixt the dark sod and the moving heavens. And oftentimes have I seen you rising to dance with the light, but I have also seen you shy. All roots are shy. They have hidden their hearts so long that they know not what to do with their hearts.

"But May shall come, and May is a restless virgin, and she shall mother the hills and plains."

AND one who had served in the Temple besought him saying: "Teach us, Master, that our words may be even as your words, a chant and an incense unto the people."

And Almustafa answered and said: "You shall rise beyond your words, but your path shall remain, a rhythm and a fragrance; a rhythm for lovers and for all who are beloved, and a fragrance for those who would live life in a garden.

"But you shall rise beyond your words to a summit whereon the star-dust falls, and you shall open your hands until they are filled; then you shall lie down and sleep like a white fledgling in a white nest, and you shall dream of your tomorrow as white violets dream of spring.

"Ay, and you shall go down deeper than your words. You shall seek the lost fountain-heads of the streams, and you shall be a hidden cave echoing the faint voices of the depths which now you do not even hear.

"You shall go down deeper than your words, ay, deeper than all sounds, to the very heart of the earth, and there you shall be alone with Him who walks also upon the Milky Way."

And after a space one of the disciples asked him,

saying: "Master, speak to us of *being*. What is it to *be*?"

And Almustafa looked long upon him and loved him. And he stood up and walked a distance away from them; then, returning, he said: "In this Garden my father and my mother lie, buried by the hands of the living; and in this Garden lie buried the seeds of yesteryear, brought hither upon the wings of the wind. A thousand times shall my mother and my father be buried here, and a thousand times shall the wind bury the seed; and a thousand years hence shall you and I and these flowers come together in this Garden even as now, and we shall *be*, loving life, and we shall *be*, dreaming of space, and we shall *be*, rising toward the sun.

"But now today to *be* is to be wise, though not a stranger to the foolish; it is to be strong, but not to the undoing of the weak; to play with young children, not as fathers, but rather as playmates who would learn their games;

"To be simple and guileless with old men and women, and to sit with them in the shade of the ancient oak-tree, though you are still walking with Spring;

"To seek a poet though he may live beyond the seven rivers, and to be at peace in his presence, nothing wanting, nothing doubting, and with no question upon your lips;

"To know that the saint and the sinner are twin brothers, whose father is our Gracious King, and that one was born but the moment before the other, wherefore we regard him as the Crowned Prince;

"To follow Beauty even when she shall lead you to the verge of the precipice; and though she is wingèd and you are wingless, and though she shall pass beyond the verge, follow her, for where Beauty is not, there is nothing;

"To be a garden without walls, a vineyard without a guardian, a treasure-house for ever open to passers-by;

"To be robbed, cheated, deceived, ay, misled and trapped and then mocked, yet with it all to look down from the height of your larger self and smile, knowing that there is a spring that will come to your garden to dance in your leaves, and an autumn to ripen your grapes; knowing that if but one of your windows is open to the East, you shall never be empty; knowing that all those deemed wrongdoers and robbers, cheaters and deceivers, are your brothers in need, and that you are perchance all of these in the eyes of the blessed inhabitants of that City Invisible, above this city.

"And now, to you also whose hands fashion and find all things that are needful for the comfort of our days and our nights——

"To *be* is to be a weaver with seeing fingers, a builder mindful of light and space; to be a plough-man and feel that you are hiding a treasure with every seed you sow; to be a fisherman and a hunter with a pity for the fish and for the beast, yet a still greater pity for the hunger and need of man.

"And, above all, I say this: I would have you each and every one partners to the purpose of every man, for only so shall you hope to obtain your own good purpose.

"My comrades and my beloved, be bold and not meek; be spacious and not confined; and until my final hour and yours be indeed your greater self."

And he ceased from speaking and there fell a deep gloom upon the nine, and their heart was turned away from him, for they understood not his words.

And behold, the three men who were mariners longed for the sea; and they who had served in the Temple yearned for the consolation of her sanctuary; and they who had been his play-fellows desired the market-place. They all were deaf to his words, so that the sound of them returned unto him like weary and homeless birds seeking refuge.

And Almustafa walked a distance from them in the Garden, saying nothing, nor looking upon them.

And they began to reason among themselves and to seek excuse for their longing to be gone.

And behold, they turned and went every man to his own place, so that Almustafa, the chosen and the beloved, was left alone.

AND when the night was fully come, he took his steps to the grave-side of his mother and sat beneath the cedar-tree which grew above the place. And there came the shadow of a great light upon the sky, and the Garden shone like a fair jewel upon the breast of earth.

And Almustafa cried out in the aloneness of his spirit, and he said:

"Heavy-laden is my soul with her own ripe fruit. Who is there would come and take and be satisfied? Is there not one who has fasted and who is kindly and generous in heart, to come and break his fast upon my first yieldings to the sun and thus ease me of the weight of mine own abundance?

"My soul is running over with the wine of the ages. Is there no thirsty one to come and drink?

"Behold, there was a man standing at the cross-roads with hands stretched forth unto the passers-by, and his hands were filled with jewels. And he called upon the passers-by, saying: 'Pity me, and take from me. In God's name, take out of my hands and console me.'

"But the passers-by only looked upon him, and none took out of his hand.

"Would rather that he were a beggar stretching

forth his hand to receive—ay, a shivering hand, and brought back empty to his bosom—than to stretch it forth full of rich gifts and find none to receive.

"And behold, there was also the gracious prince who raised up his silken tents between the mountain and the desert and bade his servants to burn fire, a sign to the stranger and the wanderer; and who sent forth his slaves to watch the road that they might fetch a guest. But the roads and the paths of the desert were unyielding, and they found no one.

"Would rather that prince were a man of nowhere and nowhen, seeking food and shelter. Would that he were the wanderer with naught but his staff and an earthen vessel. For then at nightfall would he meet with his kind, and with the poets of nowhere and nowhen, and share their beggary and their remembrances and their dreaming.

"And behold, the daughter of the great king rose from sleep and put upon her her silken raiment and her pearls and her rubies, and she scattered musk upon her hair and dipped her fingers in amber. Then she descended from her tower to her garden, where the dew of night found her golden sandals.

"In the stillness of the night the daughter of the great king sought love in the garden, but in all the vast kingdom of her father there was none who was her lover.

"Would rather that she were the daughter of a ploughman, tending his sheep in a field, and returning to her father's house at eventide with the dust of the curving roads upon her feet, and the fragrance of the vineyards in the folds of her garment. And when the night is come, and the angel of the night is upon the world, she would steal her steps to the river-valley where her lover waits.

"Would that she were a nun in a cloister burning her heart for incense, that her heart may rise to the wind, and exhausting her spirit, a candle, for a light arising toward the greater light, together with all those who worship and those who love and are beloved.

"Would rather that she were a woman ancient of years, sitting in the sun and remembering who had shared her youth."

And the night waxed deep, and Almustafa was dark with the night, and his spirit was as a cloud unspent. And he cried again:

"Heavy-laden is my soul with her own ripe fruit;
  Heavy-laden is my soul with her fruit.
  Who now will come and eat and be fulfilled?
  My soul is overflowing with her wine.
  Who now will pour and drink and be cooled of the
      desert heat?

"Would that I were a tree flowerless and fruitless,
  For the pain of abundance is more bitter than
      barrenness,
  And the sorrow of the rich from whom no one will
      take
  Is greater than the grief of the beggar to whom none
      would give.

"Would that I were a well, dry and parched, and men
          throwing stones into me;
   For this were better and easier to be borne than to
          be a source of living water
   When men pass by and will not drink.

"Would that I were a reed trodden under foot,
   For that were better than to be a lyre of silvery
          strings
   In a house whose lord has no fingers
   And whose children are deaf."

N OW, for seven days and seven nights no man came nigh the Garden, and he was alone with his memories and his pain; for even those who had heard his words with love and patience had turned away to the pursuits of other days.

Only Karima came, with silence upon her face like a veil; and with cup and plate within her hand, drink and meat for his aloneness and his hunger. And after setting these before him, she walked her way.

And Almustafa came again to the company of the white poplars within the gate, and he sat looking upon the road. And after a while he beheld as it were a cloud of dust blown above the road and coming toward him. And from out the cloud came the nine, and before them Karima guiding them.

And Almustafa advanced and met them upon the road, and they passed through the gate, and all was well, as though they had gone their path but an hour ago.

They came in and supped with him at his frugal board, after that Karima had laid upon it the bread and the fish and poured the last of the wine into the cups. And as she poured, she besought the Master, saying: "Give me leave that I go into the city and fetch wine to replenish your cups, for this is spent."

And he looked upon her, and in his eyes were a journey and a far country, and he said: "Nay, for it is sufficient unto the hour."

And they ate and drank and were satisfied. And when it was finished, Almustafa spoke in a vast voice, deep as the sea and full as a great tide under the moon, and he said: "My comrades and my road-fellows, we must needs part this day. Long have we sailed the perilous seas, and we have climbed the steepest mountains and we have wrestled with the storms. We have known hunger, but we have also sat at wedding-feasts. Oftentimes have we been naked, but we have also worn kingly raiment. We have indeed travelled far, but now we part. Together you shall go your way, and alone must I go mine.

"And though the seas and the vast lands shall separate us, still we shall be companions upon our journey to the Holy Mountain.

"But before we go our severed roads, I would give unto you the harvest and the gleaning of my heart:

"Go you upon your way with singing, but let each song be brief, for only the songs that die young upon your lips shall live in human hearts.

"Tell a lovely truth in little words, but never an ugly truth in any words. Tell the maiden whose hair shines in the sun that she is the daughter of the morning. But if you shall behold the sightless, say not to him that he is one with night.

"Listen to the flute-player as it were listening to

April, but if you shall hear the critic and the fault-finder speak, be deaf as your own bones and as distant as your fancy.

"My comrades and my beloved, upon your way you shall meet men with hoofs; give them of your wings. And men with horns; give them wreaths of laurel. And men with claws, give them petals for fingers. And men with forked tongues; give them honey for words.

"Ay, you shall meet all these and more; you shall meet the lame selling crutches; and the blind, mirrors. And you shall meet the rich men begging at the gate of the Temple.

"To the lame give of your swiftness, to the blind of your vision; and see that you give of yourself to the rich beggars; they are the most needy of all, for surely no man would stretch a hand for alms unless he be poor indeed, though of great possessions.

"My comrades and my friends, I charge you by our love that you be countless paths which cross one another in the desert, where the lions and the rabbits walk, and also the wolves and the sheep.

"And remember this of me: I teach you not giving, but receiving; not denial, but fulfilment; and not yielding, but understanding, with the smile upon the lips.

"I teach you not silence, but rather a song not over-loud.

"I teach you your larger self, which contains all men."

And he rose from the board and went out straightway into the Garden and walked under the shadow of the cypress-trees as the day waned. And they followed him, at a little distance, for their heart was heavy, and their tongue clave to the roof of their mouth.

Only Karima, after she had put by the fragments, came unto him and said: "Master, I would that you suffer me to prepare food against the morrow and your journey."

And he looked upon her with eyes that saw other worlds than this, and he said: "My sister, and my beloved, it is done, even from the beginning of time. The food and the drink is ready, for the morrow, even as for our yesterday and our today.

"I go, but if I go with a truth not yet voiced, that very truth will again seek me and gather me, though my elements be scattered throughout the silences of eternity, and again shall I come before you that I may speak with a voice born anew out of the heart of those boundless silences.

"And if there be aught of beauty that I have declared not unto you, then once again shall I be called, ay, even by mine own name, Almustafa, and I shall give you a sign, that you may know I have come back to speak all that is lacking, for God will not suffer Himself to be hidden from man, nor His word to lie covered in the abyss of the heart of man.

"I shall live beyond death, and I shall sing in your
        ears
    Even after the vast sea-wave carries me back
    To the vast sea-depth.

50

I shall sit at your board though without a body,
And I shall go with you to your fields, a spirit
  invisible.
I shall come to you at your fireside, a guest unseen.
Death changes nothing but the masks that cover
  our faces.
The woodsman shall be still a woodsman,
The ploughman, a ploughman,
And he who sang his song to the wind shall sing it
  also to the moving spheres."

And the disciples were as still as stones, and grieved
in their heart for that he had said: "I go." But no
man put out his hand to stay the Master, nor did any
follow after his footsteps.

And Almustafa went out from the Garden of his
mother, and his feet were swift and they were sound-
less; and in a moment, like a blown leaf in a strong
wind, he was far gone from them, and they saw, as
it were, a pale light moving up to the heights.

And the nine walked their ways down the road.
But the woman still stood in the gathering night, and
she beheld how the light and the twilight were become one; and she comforted her desolation and her
aloneness with his words: "I go, but if I go with a
truth not yet voiced, that very truth will seek me and
gather me, and again shall I come."

AND now it was eventide.
And he had reached the hills. His steps had led
him to the mist, and he stood among the rocks and
the white cypress-trees hidden from all things, and
he spoke and said:

"O Mist, my sister, white breath not yet held in a
      mould,
  I return to you, a breath white and voiceless,
  A word not yet uttered.

"O Mist, my wingèd sister mist, we are together
      now,
  And together we shall be till life's second day,
  Whose dawn shall lay you, dewdrops in a garden,
  And me a babe upon the breast of a woman,
  And we shall remember.

"O Mist, my sister, I come back, a heart listening in
      its depths,
  Even as your heart,
  A desire throbbing and aimless even as your desire,
  A thought not yet gathered, even as your thought.

"O Mist, my sister, first-born of my mother,
My hands still hold the green seeds you bade me
scatter,
And my lips are sealed upon the song you bade me
sing;
And I bring you no fruit, and I bring you no echoes,
For my hands were blind, and my lips unyielding.

"O Mist, my sister, much did I love the world, and
the world loved me,
For all my smiles were upon her lips, and all her
tears were in my eyes.
Yet there was between us a gulf of silence which
she would not abridge
And I could not overstep.

"O Mist, my sister, my deathless sister Mist,
I sang the ancient songs unto my little children,
And they listened, and there was wondering upon
their face;
But tomorrow perchance they will forget the song,
And I know not to whom the wind will carry the
song.
And though it was not mine own, yet it came to
my heart
And dwelt for a moment upon my lips.

"O Mist, my sister, though all this came to pass,
I am at peace.
It was enough to sing to those already born.
And though the singing is indeed not mine,
Yet it is of my heart's deepest desire.

53

"O Mist, my sister, my sister Mist,
I am one with you now.
No longer am I a self.
The walls have fallen,
And the chains have broken;
I rise to you, a mist,
And together we shall float upon the sea until life's
    second day,
When dawn shall lay you, dewdrops in a garden,
And me a babe upon the breast of a woman."